Dieter Alfter
Fotos von Günther Dächert

Bad Pyrmont

Bilder aus dem Fürstenbad

Images from the Bath of the Princes

CW Niemeyer

Blick vom Brunnenplatz über die Hauptallee auf die Untere Hauptallee mit Infozentrum
View from Brunnenplatz across Hauptallee towards Untere Hauptallee with the Infozentrum

IMPRESSUM

Bibliografische Information der Deutschen Nationalbibliothek Die Deutsche Nationalbibliothek verzeichnet diese Publikation in der Deutschen Nationalbibliografie; detaillierte bibliografische Daten sind im Internet abrufbar über http://dnb.ddb.de

Texte
Dieter Alfter, Bad Pyrmont
Fotos
Günther Dächert, Karben
S. 24, 36, 37, 71 Museum im Schloss Bad Pyrmont (außer 36 oben links)

Stadtkarte
R. Beith Design
Englische Übersetzung
Compact, Göttingen
ISBN
978-3-8271-9111-3

Printed in Germany

Quellmund der Friedrichsquelle
Spring Mouth of the Friedrichsquelle

Inhalt

Contents

Einleitung

Bad Pyrmont, niedersächsisches Staatsbad im Weserbergland, zählt zu den attraktivsten und geschichtsträchtigsten Kurorten in Deutschland. Da ist also zunächst die fast 2000 Jahre währende Geschichte. Heute überzeugt vor allen Dingen die Kompetenz Bad Pyrmonts in Sachen Gesundheit und natürliche Heilmittel. Schließlich trägt das vielfältige kulturelle und sportliche Angebot dazu bei, Seele und Leib der Kurgäste zu stärken. Gäste aus dem Weserbergland und aus dem norddeutschen Raum kommen gerade wegen des reichen Kulturangebots und der erholsamen Wandermöglichkeiten gern in das Tal der sprudelnden Quellen.

Dieses Angebot an medizinischer Kompetenz, an anspruchsvollen Freizeitmöglichkeiten hat seine besondere Geschichte. Nicht zufällig wird der bahnreisende Gast in Bad Pyrmont mit dem zusätzlichen Titel „Fürstenbad" begrüßt. In einem Tal, dessen Brodelbrunnenquelle auf dem heutigen Brunnenplatz im 1–4. Jahrhundert von Germanen durch kostbare Opfergaben, heute bekannt als Pyrmonter Brunnenfund, verehrt wurde. Es dauerte bis in die Zeit der Renaissance und des Frühbarock, bis sich der Badeort Schritt für Schritt zu einem mondänen Treffpunkt entwickelte mit dem Ziel, adelige und vermögende bürgerliche Gästen an den Ort zu binden.

Es ist erstaunlich, welche hochrangigen Persönlichkeiten auf Initiative der Fürstenfamilie zu Waldeck und Pyrmont nach 1668 den Weg nach Pyrmont gefunden haben. Von Anfang an ging es nicht allein um die Heilwirkung der Quellen, sondern ebenso um das gesellschaftliche Ereignis. „Sehen und gesehen werden" war das Motto. 1681 begann mit dem „Fürstensommer" die glanzvolle Zeit des Badeortes. Die Welfen, vor allen Dingen Kurfürst Ernst August von Hannover, waren in der 2. Hälfte des 17. Jahrhunderts die prägende Adelsfamilie. Zar Peter der Große (1716) erweckte allerorten große Neugier, Friedrich der Große bestimmte während seiner Aufenthalte 1744 und 1746 das Kurgeschehen, Benjamin Franklin (1766), Johann Wolfgang von Goethe (1801) oder die einzigartige preußische Königin Luise, die Pyrmont als Kind (1777), als Kronprinzessin (1796) und als Königin (1806) besuchte, sind nur einige Glanzlichter der Pyrmonter Badegesellschaft. Wahrhaftig, im 18. Jahrhundert ein Bad von europäischem Rang.

Deutlich spiegelt sich das Leben der Gäste von Pyrmont wider in Briefen, in Tagebucheintragungen und natürlich in Büchern jener Zeit. Von vorzüglicher Qualität sind aber auch die Graphiken, die Pyrmont in Bildern vorstellen. Die Augsburger Guckkastenblätter waren beste Werbeträger für den Ort. Ein in Mainz im Jahre 1790 verlegter Kupferstich gibt bei genauerer Betrachtung Auskunft über das sommerliche Leben in Pyrmont. Prägend ist das Alleensystem. Die Grundstruktur dazu wurde bereits ab 1667 angelegt.

Der Brunnenplatz mit seinen Quellen ist der Mittelpunkt Pyrmonts. Alles ist

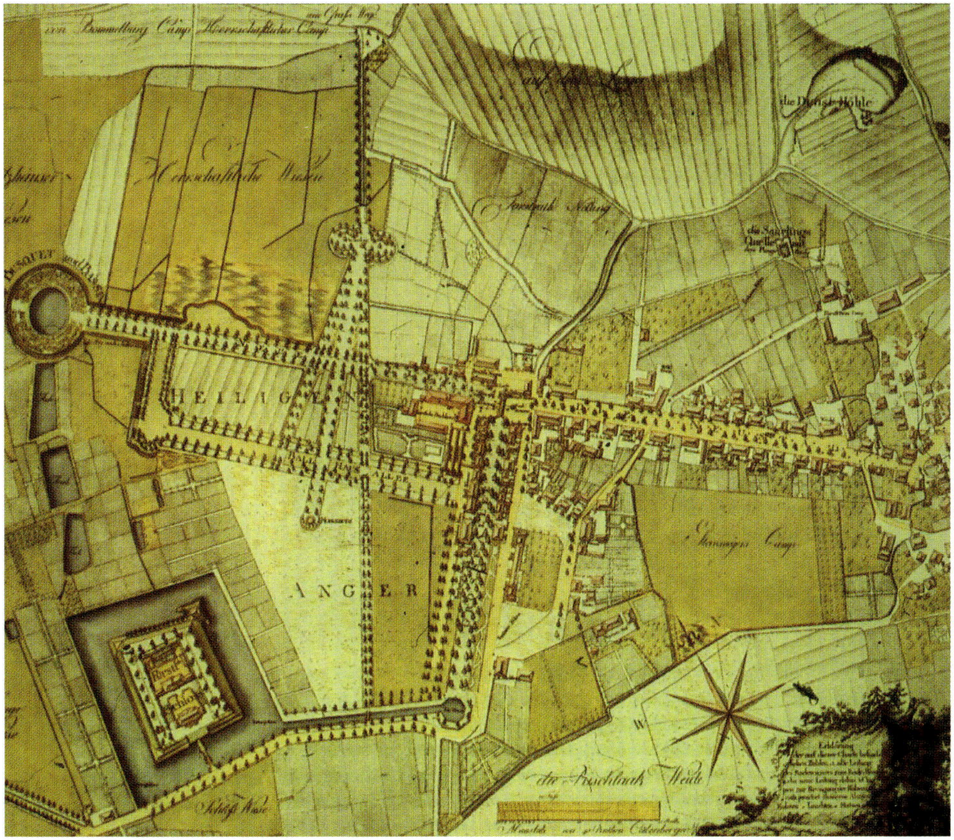

darauf ausgerichtet, auch die Hauptallee. Dieser „Spatziergang“ diente der Therapie in Form von Bewegung, war aber auch eine Bühne, ein Treffpunkt für die Badegesellschaft.

Die heutige Brunnenstraße diente in jener Zeit als Logierstraße. Ein Blick von der Fontäne über den Kanal führte in Richtung Festung und Schloss, dem Sommersitz der Fürsten zu Waldeck und Pyrmont. Das Alleensystem dient bis auf den heutigen Tag den traditionell typischen Angeboten des Badeortes: Kur-Natur-Kultur. Wer Bad Pyrmont heute besucht, wird noch immer den Dreiklang dieser Worte fühlen, wird immer noch – wie vor Jahrhunderten – das besondere Flair und die Eleganz des Ortes wahrnehmen. Der Gast ist nicht nur an der Quelle der Gesundheit, er spürt und genießt auch das anspruchsvolle Freizeitangebot.

Gesamtansicht von Pyrmont, 1790. Kupferstich von Dammert und Cöntgen, Mainz
General view of Pyrmont, 1790. Copperplate engraving by Dammert and Cöntgen, Mainz

Fürstliches Badelogierhaus, das vornehmste Hotel am Brunnenplatz, erbaut 1777–1778, finanziert durch eine niederländische Aktiengesellschaft. Hier logierten viele vornehme Gäste, so Königin Luise von Preußen, Fürst Hardenberg, Fürst Blücher oder König Willem III. der Niederlande.
The Fürstliches Badelogierhaus (‘Princes’ Bathing Lodge’), the most elegant hotel on the Brunnenplatz, built 1777–1778 with funds from a Dutch corporation. Many guests of noble birth took lodgings here, such as Queen Luise of Prussia, Prince Hardenberg, Prince Blücher or King William III of the Netherlands.

Introduction

Bad Pyrmont, state-recognised spa in the Weser Mountains, Lower Saxony, is among the most attractive and historically fascinating spa towns in Germany. Not only almost 2000 years of history have given the town its character, but in recent times especially also Bad Pyrmont's convincing competence in all matters of health and natural medicine. After all, the amazingly varied range of cultural and sports offers contributes to sustaining body and soul of staying guests. Visitors from the Weser Mountain region and even from all over northern Germany like coming to the 'valley of gushing springs' particularly because of its rich cultural programme and the refreshing hiking offers.

Such a range of medical competence and high standards of leisure activities have their particular history. It is not by accident that guests arriving in Bad Pyrmont by railway see the additional title 'Fürstenbad' ('Bath of Princes') on the sign welcoming them. In a valley where the 'Brodelbrunnen' spring was worshipped by ancient Germans during the 1st – 4th century, with precious sacrificial offerings excavated as the so-called 'Pyrmonter Brunnenfund', it took until the age of Renaissance and early Baroque for the bathing place to be developed and marketed systematically as a mundane resort with the aim of convincing guests from among the aristocracy and wealthy bourgeoisie to establish ties to the place.

It is surprising which high-ranking personages have found their way to the 'valley of gushing springs' since 1668 by initiative of the princely family of Waldeck und Pyrmont. From the very beginning, the focus of attention was not on the curative effects of the springs alone, but also on the stay as a social event. The motto was 'See and Be Seen'. In 1681, in what became known as the 'Fürstensommer', the 'Summer of the Princes', the glorious days of the spa began. During the second half of the 17th century, the family of the Guelphs, in particular Elector Ernst August of Hanover, gave character to the place as visitors. Tsar Peter the Great aroused everybody's curiosity in 1716, Frederick the Great domi-

Wandelhalle und Brunnenplatz bilden den Mittelpunkt des traditionsreichen Badeortes. Der Brunnentempel wie die Wandelhalle wurden von Preußen 1923–24 erbaut auf den Fundamenten der beiden Vorgängerbauten aus dem 17. beziehungsweise 19. Jahrhundert.
The Wandelhalle (ambulatory) and the Brunnenplatz form the very centre of the spa town rich in tradition. The Brunnentempel and the Wandelhalle were constructed by the state of Prussia in 1923–24, on the foundations of two earlier buildings dating back to the 17th and 19th century respectively.

nated the life of the spa town during his two stays in 1744 and 1746, Benjamin Franklin (1766), Johann Wolfgang von Goethe (1801) or the remarkable Luise, Queen of Prussia, visiting Pyrmont as a child (1777), as Crown Princess (1796) and Queen (1806), are only a few social highlights of the spa society of Pyrmont. Truly a spa of Europe-wide renown in the 18th century.

The life of the guests to Bad Pyrmont is reflected in detail in letters, diary entries, and of course in books published at the time. The range of prints showing Pyrmont in pictures is also of excellent quality. The 'Guckkastenblätter' from Augsburg are an effective means of the time of advertising the place. A closer look at a copperplate print published in 1790 in Mainz reveals details of summer life in Pyrmont. A characteristic feature is the system of avenues, established as early as 1667.

The Brunnenplatz ('Fountain Square') with its springs is the centre of Pyrmont. Everything is arranged in its direction, including the main avenue, the 'Hauptallee'. This 'Spatziergang' ('Promenade') was intended for therapy by means of movement, yet was also a stage, a meeting place for the spa society.

What nowadays is named Brunnenstrasse used to be a street of lodgings. There was a view from the fountain along the canal towards the castle and palace, the summer residence of the Princes of Waldeck und Pyrmont. Up to the present day, the system of avenues is dedicated to the traditional, typical features of the spa town: Cure – Nature – Culture. Visiting Bad Pyrmont today, you will find that these three words still sound harmoniously here, and you will perceive the particular flair and elegance of the place, just as it was centuries ago. Not only are you close to the fountain of health, you will also get into the feeling and pleasure of the range of sophisticated leisure offers.

Der Palmengarten: Die ersten zwölf Phönix-Palmen wurden im Mai 1912 aufgestellt.

The Palmengarten (Palm Garden): the first twelve Phoenix plams were placed in May, 1912.

Fotografien aus einem Sportflugzeug auf das Pyrmonter Tal erzählen von der heute noch so sorgsam gepflegten Kulturlandschaft um die Parkanlagen und Quellen Bad Pyrmonts. Das barocke Achsensystem aus der Zeit des 18. Jahrhunderts ist ebenso prägend wie das Element des Landschaftsgartens im engeren Kurbezirk als auch im Bergkurpark. Nach wie vor nehmen die Pensionshäuser Bezug auf den Naturraum und verstehen sich in erster Linie als Beherbergungsmöglichkeiten für ruhe- und erholungsuchende Gäste.

Photos of the Pyrmont Valley, taken from a sports plane, tell a tale of the – still carefully tended - cultivated landscape surrounding the park areas and springs of Bad Pyrmont. The baroque-style system of axes dating back to the 18th century is as much a distinct feature as the elements of landscape gardening in the inner spa district as well as in the Bergkurpark. Even today, the guesthouses maintain their reference to the open space of nature and are primarily considered places of lodging for guests seeking rest and tranquillity.

Das Kurzentrum
The Kurzentrum

Der Brunnenplatz ist das Herzstück des Kurzentrums. Der Hyllige Born und der Brodelbrunnen, aber auch der Augenbrunnen sind drei markante Quellen dieses Platzes, zu dem ursprünglich noch zwei weitere Säuerlingsquellen zählten. Auf diesem Platz traf sich seit dem 17. Jahrhundert die vornehme Badegesellschaft. Am frühen Morgen ließ man sich das Heilwasser zureichen, von hier bewegte sich die Gesellschaft die Hauptallee auf und ab und wiederholte dies mehrfach am Tag.

Brunnenplatz is the heart of the Kurzentrum. Three distinctive springs originate from this square, the Hyllige Born and the Brodelbrunnen, and also the Augenbrunnen, with originally yet a further two mineral springs. Since the 17th century, this has been the meeting place of noble society at the spa. The medicinal waters were served here in the early morning, and from here, parties moved up and down the Hauptallee (main avenue), repeating the procedure several times a day.

1999 wurde die in den Zwanziger Jahren erbaute Wandelhalle renoviert – die Marmorskulptur der Königin Luise stammt von dem Berliner Bildhauer Emil Hundrieser. Heute begrüßt sie die Gäste. Als Gläser- und Wasserausgabe erfüllt die Wandelhalle immer noch die wichtigste Funktion dieses Gebäudes, aber Cafés und Boutiquen waren von Anfang an Teil der Neugestaltung der Wandelhalle.

In 1999, the Wandelhalle (Ambulatory) built in the 1920s was renovated – the marble sculpture of Queen Luise is by Berlin sculptor Emil Hundrieser. Today, it welcomes arriving guests. As the central location to distribute glasses and water, the Wandelhalle still serves its original function, but from the beginning, cafés and boutiques were intended as part of the design for the renovated Ambulatory.

Die Hauptallee, ab 1667 von zwei bayerischen, im Dienste Arolsens stehenden Gärtnern geplant und angelegt, diente zunächst einmal der Bewegung. Der „Spatziergang" war eine der ältesten Fußgängeranlagen in Deutschland. Das schluckweise Trinken des heilkräftigen Wassers beim Flanieren unter den schattigen Lindenbäumen war als Therapieangebot zu verstehen. Die Allee selbst mit ihren Boutiquen, Gasthäusern, Ballsälen, Musik- und Theaterdarbietungen war die ideale Bühne für das gesellschaftliche Ereignis einer Kur.

Die Hauptallee war zugleich ein beliebter Ort der Kommunikation, um private Kontakte zu knüpfen oder um einen Gedankenaustausch zu pflegen. Heute erinnert der Verein „Historischer Fürstentreff e.V." alljährlich am ersten Juliwochenende an die glanzvolle Zeit Pyrmonts als Treffpunkt des europäischen Hochadels.

The Hauptallee (Main Avenue), planned and executed from 1667 on by two Bavarian gardeners in the service of the town of Arolsen, had the primary purpose of animating guests to walk. The 'Spatziergang' ('Promenade') is one of the oldest pedestrian-only facilities in Germany. The slow sipping of medicinal water while taking a stroll under shady linden trees was to be considered therapeutic treatment. The avenue itself with its shops, taverns, ballrooms, musical and theatrical performances was a perfect stage to celebrate a course of treatment as a social event.

The Hauptallee was also a popular place of communication, to make contact in a private atmosphere or to exchange thoughts and ideas.

Today, the association 'Historischer Fürstentreff e.V.' anually, on the first July weekend, commemorates the glorious days of Pyrmont as a meeting place for the European high nobility.

KURTHEATER

In Bad Pyrmont verbinden sich Vergangenheit und Gegenwart. Ist das altehrwürdige Kurtheater noch Sinnbild für die Biedermeierzeit des frühen 19. Jahrhunderts, so bietet das Steigenberger Hotel Bad Pyrmont hinter der Fassade des alten Kurhauses jeden erdenklichen Komfort, jede persönliche Erholung für Leib und Seele. Die Büste von Albert Lortzing erinnert an die Auftritte dieses Komponisten als Schauspieler und Sänger in den Jahren 1827–1833.

Bad Pyrmont is a place where history and modernity blend well. While the venerable Kurtheater remains a symbol of the Biedermeier era in the earlier 19th century, the Steigenberger Hotel Bad Pyrmont, established behind the facade of the old Kurhaus, offers every imaginable aspect of comfort and personal relaxation for body and soul. The bust of Albert Lortzing commemorates the composer's performances in town as an actor and singer in the years 1827–1833.

Das Lesesaalgebäude und die Arkaden mit individuellen Geschäften grenzen die Hauptallee vom Kurpark ab. Der Titel des Haupteinganges „Brandenburger Tor" erinnert an Berlin und Preußen. Der preußische Staat finanzierte ab 1922 die architektonische Neugestaltung des Kurzentrums. Der Endpunkt der historischen Hauptallee ist ein nach den Entwürfen von Peter Szaif entworfener Brunnen, der das Wasser als Sinnbild für die Pyrmonter Heilquellen in einer Art Vorhang über drei Bronzeschalen in das Brunnenbecken fließen lässt.
The building of the Lesesaal (reading room) and the arcades with individual shops separate the Hauptallee and the Kurpark. The name of the main entrance gate, 'Brandenburg Gate', is a reminder of Berlin and Prussia. From 1922, the Prussian state provided the funding to architectually redesign the Kurzentrum. The end point of the historic Hauptallee ist now a fountain designed by Peter Szaif where, symbolic of the medicinal springs of Pyrmont, water flows down in a kind of curtain over three bronze bowls into the fountain pool.

Der Weltausstellung Expo 2000 in Hannover ist es zu verdanken, dass die historische Hauptallee nun um eine Achse bis zum Informationszentrum verlängert werden konnte. Seit diesem Zeitpunkt flaniert der Besucher über eine moderne Allee, begleitet von dem sprudelnden Geräusch des Wasserlaufs, von Musik und von Skulpturen des Bildhauers Jürgen Goertz. Sie stellen einerseits den Lebenslauf der Menschen von der Kindheit bis ins hohe Alter dar, andererseits erzählen die Figuren die Geschichte der Menschheit von den Anfängen bis in die Gegenwart.

Thanks to the world exhibition Expo 2000 in Hannover, it was possible to extend the historic Hauptallee by one axis as far as the Informationszentrum. Since then, visitors can stroll along a modern avenue, accompanied on the way by music, by the bubbly sound of running water, and works of art by sculptor Jürgen Goertz. On the one hand, the sculptures depict the course of human life from childhood to old age, while on the other hand telling the story of humankind from its beginnings to the present day.

Am Ende dieser langen Achse befindet sich das Tourist-Informationszentrum, die erste Anlaufstelle für jeden Gast. Hier laufen in der Bad Pyrmont Tourismus GmbH alle Fäden der Vermarktung zusammen. Erscheinungsbild und Grundform dieses Gebäudes aus Glas und Stahl nehmen die Architektur des Brunnentempels über der Hylligen Born-Quelle in moderner Form wieder auf.

At the end of this prolonged axis, the Tourist-Informationszentrum is situated, the first place to go to for every guest. Here, at Bad Pyrmont Tourismus GmbH, lies the heart of all marketing activities. The outer appearance and basic shape of this glass-and-steel building recreate the architecture of the fountain temple above the Hylligen Born spring in a modern style.

Der Blick zurück über die Untere Hauptallee auf die lindenbestandene historische Hauptallee und auf den Brunnenplatz unterstreicht, in welchem Gleichklang und in welcher Vielfalt Natur, Kultur und Kur hier zusammenwirken. Diese Achse ist der Lebensnerv des Kurortes, von der nach einem festgelegten, aus der Barockzeit stammenden Plans weitere Achsen ausgehen.

A look back along the Untere Hauptallee towards the historic Hauptallee lined by linden trees and towards Brunnenplatz once more shows the harmony and variety of 'Cure, Culture and Nature' working in unison here. This axis is the spa town's life nerve, with secondary axes branching off according to a fixed plan dating back to the Baroque era.

Am Ende der historischen Hauptallee konnte man früher den Blick genießen von der Fontäne über einen Kanal und über die Graft zu Festung und Schloss Pyrmont. Heute sind es die Schlossstraße, das Konzerthaus und die nach Königin Emma benannte Grünfläche, die den Blick lenken.

The view one used to enjoy from the fountain at the end of the historic Hauptallee was across a canal and the moat towards Pyrmont Castle and Palace. Today, the sights to catch the beholder's eye are Schlossstraße, the concert hall and the green named after Queen Emma.

Das Konzerthaus, ein beeindruckendes Gebäude der Zwanziger Jahre mit Stilelementen des Art déco, ist geradezu ein Sinnbild für das berühmte Musikbad Pyrmont. Welches große Orchester, welcher namhafte Dirigent oder Solist hat nicht in diesem akustisch so bemerkenswerten Haus gespielt!

The Konzerthaus (concert hall), an impressive construction of the 1920s with elements of art déco style, has become almost a symbol of the 'Musical Spa' Pyrmont. What great orchestra, what renowned conductor or soloist is there who has not performed in this acoustically most remarkable hall!

Festung und Schloss
Pyrmont Castle and Palace

Festung und Schloss Pyrmont , in der Renaissance ehemals eine trutzige, von einer Graft umgebenen Festungsanlage, dann von 1706–1710 überbaut zu der barocken Sommerresidenz der Fürsten zu Waldeck und Pyrmont, sind heute eine vielfältig genutzte Kulturinsel. Das Schloss beherbergt die stadt- und badgeschichtliche Sammlung des Museums im Schloss, präsentiert aber auch mit großem Erfolg Sonderausstellungen in den Räumen der Beletage. Die Kreisvolkshochschule befindet sich in den Räumen des Kommandantenhauses. Die vom Staatsbad veranstalteten Open-Air-Ereignisse in dem großen wie im kleinen Schlosshof sind während der Sommermonate von größter Attraktivität. Es gibt in Bad Pyrmont keinen Veranstaltungsort, der alle Künste von Theater und Musik, von Kabarett und Kleinkunst bis zu den bildenden Künsten auf einer Anlage miteinander verknüpft. Bemerkenswert ist die einzigartige Kulisse.

Pyrmont Castle and Palace, originally a fortress surrounded by a moat which up until the Renaissance defied attackers, was reconstructed 1706–1710 to become the baroque-style summer residence of the Princes of Waldeck und Pyrmont, and today serves as an island of culture for a great variety of occasions. The palace houses the collection of town and spa history of the palace museum, yet its bel-étage rooms are also very successfully used as a venue for special exhibitions. In the rooms of the Kommandantenhaus, the district adult education centre is located. During the summer months, the open air events in the large and the smaller palace courtyard hosted by the spa town are a great attraction. There is no other venue in Bad Pyrmont where all the arts, from theatre and music via comedy and variety to graphic and visual arts can be gathered and combined in one place, before the magnificent background of the architectural ensemble established over a number of centuries.

Das Museum beherbergt kostbare Kunstwerke aus der Vergangenheit Pyrmonts. Den Ausgangspunkt bildet der Pyrmonter Brunnenfund, sehenswert sind Badegläser und Porzellane mit Ansichten Pyrmonts. Zwei außergewöhnliche Kratervasen aus dem Besitz von Dr. Hufeland erinnern an den Badeaufenthalt von Königin Luise. Im Musensalon, ausgestattet von den Kasseler Hofmalern J. H. Tischbein und F. A. Tischbein, kann heute auch standesamtlich geheiratet werden. Die Beletage wird genutzt für Ausstellungen des Museums, für Kammerkonzerte, Vorträge und festliche Empfänge.

The Museum houses precious works of art from Pyrmont's history. Starting point is the 'Pyrmonter Brunnenfund' , the spa water glasses and porcelain objects with views of Pyrmont are worth seeing. Two extraordinary krater vases formerly owned by Dr. Hufeland are reminders of the days when Queen Luise stayed to take the waters. In the 'Musensalon', ceremonially opened in 1777, decorated by Kassel court painters J. H. Tischbein und F. A. Tischbein, it is nowadays possible to have marriage registration ceremonies. The bel-étage is used for the more complex exhibitions of the museum as well as for chamber concerts, lectures and receptions.

Während der Sommermonate bewohnte die Fürstenfamilie zu Waldeck und Pyrmont das Schloss. Das Kommandantenhaus wurde ganzjährig von einem hohen Beamten aus der Residenzstadt Arolsen als Verwaltungssitz genutzt. Für die Bewohner der kleinen Grafschaft diente das schlichte zweigeschossige Haus als eine Art Rathaus. Heute finden in diesen Räumen die Veranstaltungen der VHS Hameln-Pyrmont statt.

During the summer months, the princely family of Waldeck und Pyrmont resided in the palace. The 'Kommandantenhaus' was used around the year by a high-ranking official from the residency town of Arolsen as an administrative seat. To the population of the small county, the plain two-storey building served as a kind of town hall. Today, the premises are used for adult education classes of the Volkshochschule Hameln-Pyrmont.

Vor der Kulisse der barocken Schlossgebäude, aber auch vor dem Hintergrund der Festungsmauern aus der Zeit der Renaissance erleben die Besucher einzigartige Freiluftveranstaltungen. Die besondere Atmosphäre der Konzerte und Theateraufführungen sind Teil eines traumhaften Kulturangebots während der Sommersaison. Große Schirme sind nicht nur bei Regenwetter hilfreich, sie verwandeln diesen Außenraum in einen ungewöhnlichen Innenraum.

Before the background of the baroque palace buildings, but also of the fortress walls dating back to the Renaissance, visitors experience unforgettable open-air events. The particular atmosphere of the concerts and theatre performances is part of a fabulous cultural programme during the summer season. Large umbrellas are not only useful in case of rainy weather, they also transform the open-air expanse into an extraordinary interior.

Originally, the fortress construction begun in 1526 was part of the residence of the counts of Spiegelberg, who in times of war were able to provide their subjects from the county's ten villages with protection inside their large castle courtyard. Even during the 30-Year War, the massive fortifications behind a wide moat, high ramparts and a corner bastion were not taken by military force, yet forced to capitulate several times due to starvation after a siege of the bridge.

Ursprünglich war die ab 1526 erbaute Festungsanlage Teil eines Herrschaftssitzes der Grafen von Spiegelberg, die in kriegerischen Zeiten ihren Untertanen aus den zehn Dörfern der Grafschaft in dem großen Schlosshof sicheren Schutz geben konnten. Selbst in der Zeit des Dreißigjährigen Krieges wurde die mächtige Anlage hinter dem breiten Wassergraben, hinter den hohen Wällen und der Eckbastion militärisch nicht erobert, allerdings mehrfach durch Belagerung der Brücke ausgehungert und zur Kapitulation gezwungen.

Der Kurpark – Tal der sprudelnden Quellen
The Kurpark – Valley of Gushing Springs

Von der Wallanlage der Festung hat man nicht nur interessante Eindrücke von der architektonischen Gesamtanlage, sondern man genießt auch den Blick auf verschiedene Landschaftsbilder und Epochen der Gartenkunst, die sich auf dem Gelände des Kurparks harmonisch miteinander verbinden. Die barocken Alleen mit ihren mächtigen Bäumen und ihren Sichtachsen bilden den historischen Hintergrund für einen schattigen Weg in der Natur. Diese Wege sollten schon im 18. Jahrhundert Flaniermöglichkeiten nach dem Vorbild der Hauptallee erweitern.

Nowadays, the fortress premises are a popular place to go for walks. From the ramparts, not only interesting impressions of the overall architectural design can be gained, there is also an enjoyable view of the different landscape scenes and eras of the art of gardening in a harmonious blend in the Kurpark. The baroque avenues with their magnificent trees and their axes of perspective provide a historic background to a pleasantly shady walk in nature. These paths provide variety to promenading, modelled on the main avenue.

Im Lauf des 19. Jahrhunderts wird auch in Bad Pyrmont der neuen Mode in der Gartenkunst Rechnung getragen. Der Englische Garten wird fester Bestandteil des Kurparks, vermittelt dem Betrachter den Eindruck einer natürlich gewachsenen Landschaft. Zugleich wird er Gast einer Parkszenerie, die den Charakter eines Bühnenbildes hat.

In the course of the 19th century, new fashions in landscape gardening are considered also in Bad Pyrmont. The English Garden becomes a permanent segment of the Kurpark, giving the beholder the impression of a naturally grown landscape. At the same time, the visitor becomes part of a park scenery representing a kind of stage.

Von der östlichen Wallkrone des Schlosses hat man einen wundervollen Blick auf den Palmengarten. Angelegt vom Hofgartendirektor Werner Dirks entwickelt er sich ab 1913 mehr und mehr zu dem wohl beliebtesten Element des Kurparks. Der Palmengarten erfüllte viele Jahrzehnte die Sehnsucht der Besucher nach einer Reise zum Mittelmeer.

From the crown of the eastern ramparts of the palace, the view of the palm garden is wonderful. It was begun by court garden director Werner Dirks, and after 1913 slowly became the probably most popular element of the Kurpark. For many decades, the 'Palmengarten' fulfilled its visitors' desire for a trip to the Mediterranean.

Seite 33: Gegenüber vom Palmengarten, von der Wallkrone der Festung, in westlicher Richtung, blickt man hinüber auf den neu gestalteten japanischen Bambusgarten. Auf dem ehemaligen Gelände des Refugiums sind nun Grundelemente der asiatischen Landschaftsauffassung ein Teil des Kurparks. Der Bad Pyrmonter Kurpark ist ein besonderes Schmuckstück, der 2005 als Deutschlands schönster Park ausgezeichnet wurde. Das 17 Hektar große Gelände ist Naturerlebnis und Ruhezone zugleich.

Page 33: Opposite the palm garden, from a position on the fortress's rampart crown facing west, one gets a look at the newly designed Japanese-style bamboo garden. On the premises of the former Refugium, one will find now basic elements of Japanese landscaping philosophy as part of the Kurpark. The Kurpark of Bad Pyrmont is an extraordinary gem which was awarded the title of Germany's most beautiful park in 2005. The 17-hectare expanse is a perfect place to experience nature and find rest at the same time.

Der Kurpark spricht als Gesamtkunstwerk alle Sinne an. Der Park ist auch die Kulisse für eindrucksvolle Freiluft-Veranstaltungen. Neben dem traditionsreichen „Goldenen Sonntag“ haben andere Veranstaltungen wie „Die Landpartie“, „Kleines Fest im großen Kurpark“ oder „Historischer Fürstentreff“ einen großen Freundeskreis gefunden.

The Kurpark has been given its character by various cultures and eras, and as such a synthesis, it stimulates all the senses. The park is also a venue for splendid open-air events. Apart from the traditional ‘Goldener Sonntag’, other events such as ‘Die Landpartie’, ‘Kleines Fest im großen Kurpark’ or ‘Historischer Fürstentreff’ have found a large circle of enthusiasts.

Die Brunnenstraße, 1720 ernannt zur Neustadt Pyrmont, war ein Angebot für anspruchsvolle Kurgäste, standesgemäß in der Nähe der Quellen zu logieren. Tatsächlich hat diese Logierstraße, die heutige Brunnenstraße, exakt die gleiche Länge wie die Hauptallee. Namhafte Gäste haben hier und in benachbarten Straßen gewohnt – Zar Peter der Große (1716), der preußische König Friedrich der Große (1744 und 1746) und der englische König Georg I. (ab 1681 bis 1716), auch Johann Gottfried Herder (ab 1772–1777), Benjamin Franklin (1766) oder Johann Wolfgang von Goethe (1801).

Brunnenstraße, the street established in 1720 under the name Neustadt Pyrmont, is an offer to the discriminating spa guest to find lodgings in style directly near the fountains. This street of lodges is of exactly the same length as the main avenue, Hauptallee. Famous guests have stayed here – Tsar Peter the Great (1716), Prussian King Frederick the Great (1744 and 1746) or George I, King of England (between 1681 and 1716), but also Johann Gottfried Herder (between 1772 and 1777), Benjamin Franklin (1766) or Johann Wolfgang von Goethe (1801).

Zar Peter der Große (oben/above)

Benjamin Franklin

Seite 37 oben / Page 37 top right
Friedrich der Große
Johann Wolfgang von Goethe

Seite 38ff. Heute ist die Brunnenstraße eine elegante Flaniermeile mit unterschiedlichsten Einkaufsmöglichkeiten, aber auch mit Restaurants und Cafés, Geldinstituten, Apotheken sowie Praxisräumen für Anwälte, Ärzte und Steuerbüros. Nur wenige Hotels wie das Haus Hemmerich und Pensionen erinnern an die vergangenen Zeiten. Die Alte Hofapotheke, im 18. Jahrhundert noch ein Ladengeschäft auf dem Brunnenplatz, ist seit Generationen die älteste Apotheke im Zentrum des Badeortes. Sie ergänzt die natürlichen Heilmittel der Pyrmonter Quellen. Diese Quellen werden in Gestalt von 19 Keramikgefäßen entlang eines blauen Bandes visualisiert.

Page 38ff. Today, Brunnenstraße is an elegant promenade with a great variety of shops as well as restaurants and cafés, banks, chemist's shops, doctors' practices, lawyers' and accountants' offices. Only a few hotels and guesthouses remain as reminders of former times. The Alte Hofapotheke, which in the 18th century still was a different kind of shop on Brunnenplatz, has been a chemist's shop for generations, the oldest one in the centre of town. It provides remedies in addition to the natural curative powers of Pyrmont's medicinal waters – which are visualised here in the form of 19 ceramic vessels along a blue ribbon.

Königin Emma
Königin Luise
(links/left)

Brunnenstraße Nordseite
Brunnenstraße northern

CITY CENTER

Der Augenoptiker

SCHWAGER

COMMERZBANK
P

SCHWAGER

Steinmeyer
Hotel
Café

Brunnenstraße Südseite
Brunnenstraße southern

IhrPlatz

IhrPlatz

Schuhpark

Cordes

Die Heilquellen von Bad Pyrmont sind überhaupt der Grund, warum Pyrmont sich seit dem Spätmittelalter zum „Tal der sprudelnden Quellen“ entwickeln konnte. Im Lauf der Historie lassen sich auf Grund der einzigartigen geologischen Bedingungen 19 Heilquellen lokalisieren. Die 5 Quellen auf dem Brunnenplatz sind bereits vorgestellt – nun kommen in östlicher und westlicher Richtung folgende wichtige Quellen hinzu: Bergsäuerlingsquelle, Eichenkellerquelle, Trampelsche Quelle, in westlicher Richtung die Helenenquelle und die Friedrichsquelle.

The medicinal springs of Bad Pyrmont are the very reason why Pyrmont has developed into the ‘Valley of Gushing Springs’ since the late middle ages. Due to the specific geological conditions, over the course of history, a total of 19 medicinal springs have been located. The 5 springs on Brunnenplatz have already been introduced – let us now add the following significant springs towards the east and west: Bergsäuerlingsquelle, Eichenkellerquelle, Trampelsche Quelle, and in a westerly direction Helenenquelle and Friedrichsquelle.

Die heilbringenden Quellen sind der Schatz von Pyrmont. Seit dem Opferfund am Brodelbrunnen auf dem Brunnenplatz, seit dem spektakulären Wundergeläuf zum Hylligen Born im Jahr 1556 hat die Magie der Heilkraft dieser Quellen nie nachgelassen. Einzigartig ist auch im Rahmen dieser geologischen Besonderheiten die Dunsthöhle. An dieser Stelle strömt durch Erdspalten und Risse aus großer Tiefe reines Kohlendioxyd, ohne dass auf dem Weg an die Erdoberfläche Tiefengrundwasser mitgenommen wird. Der Brunnenarzt Dr. Johann Philipp Seip untersuchte 1712 die Dunsthöhle, ließ sie in dem ehemaligen Steinbruch 1720 fassen und suchte nach Therapiemöglichkeiten.

The health-promoting springs are Pyrmont's treasure. Since the discovery of the Germanic sacrificial offerings, since the spectacular 'Wundergeläuf' to the Hylligen Born spring in 1556, the magic healing power of these springs has never faded. A further unique phenomenon among all these particular geological features is the 'Dunsthöhle' ('hazy cave'). In this place, pure carbon dioxide streams up through cracks and crevices from great depths, without any ground water being drawn from deep down to the surface along with it. Well doctor Johann Philipp Seip examined the Dunsthöhle in the former quarry in 1712, had a tap installed in 1720 and began to look for forms of therapy.

Naturmerkwürdigkeiten prägen auch andernorts das Bild vom Kurzentrum. Sehenswert sind unbedingt die Erdfälle. Oberhalb von Holzhausen kann man auf zwei verschiedenen Ebenen große, mit Wasser gefüllte Trichter bewundern, die durch das Auswaschen von Salzschichten durch Wasser ausgehöhlt wurden.

There are other spots of the Kurzentrum where oddities of nature can be found. A sight worth seeing are the 'Erdfälle' ('Earth Falls'). Above Holzhausen, at two levels, there are large water-filled funnels hollowed out by water washing out layers of salt.

Therapieeinrichtungen
Therapeutic Establishments

Die Naturmerkwürdigkeiten Dunsthöhle und Erdfälle liegen bereits leicht außerhalb des Kurzentrums. Am Übergang der städtischen Bebauung finden sich heute auch die Mehrzahl der Kureinrichtungen, die ein unterschiedliches und vielfältiges Therapieangebot unterbreiten. Die Hufelandtherme ist besonders beliebt.

The natural phenomena 'Dunsthöhle' and 'Erdfälle' are already slightly outside the area of the Kurzentrum. Also nowadays situated on the border to the urban, built-up area are the majority of medical cure establishments providing a great variety and diversity of therapy offers. The Hufelandtherme is especially popular.

In westlicher Richtung unmittelbar anschließend befindet sich die Klinik „Der Fürstenhof“ (oben). Das 1777 gegründete „Fürstliche Badelogierhaus“ ist heute eine Fachklinik für Stoffwechselkrankheiten des Skelettsystems. Gerade in diesem Haus wird die Bedeutung der Heilquellen mit großer Ernsthaftigkeit genutzt. Nicht weit davon entfernt, bereits an der Achse des Dreialleenblicks, befindet sich das Therapiezentrum „Königin Luise Bad“ (unten). Es ist das Gesundheitszentrum des Staatsbades Pyrmont.

Directly adjacent to the west, the Klinik 'Der Fürstenhof' (above) is situated. Today, the former princely lodge built in 1777 ('Fürstliche Badelogierhaus') is a specialist clinic for metabolic disorders of the skeletal system. At this establishment in particular, the importance of the medicinal springs is taken very seriously. And not far away, already on the axis of the three-avenue point of view, the therapy centre 'Königin Luise Bad' (below) can be found. This is the health centre of the state-recognised spa of Bad Pyrmont.

Oberhalb des Kurzentrums, in nördlicher Richtung zwischen Bergkurpark und Hirschpark gelegen, befinden sich am Fuße des Bombergs zwei namhafte Kliniken: Die Psychosomatische Fachklinik (oben) liegt unmittelbar an der Bombergallee und nutzt die vielfältigen Therapieangebote für das seelische Wohlbefinden. Die Klinik Dr. Otto Buchinger (unten), rechts der Bombergallee gelegen, wird in dritter Generation nun von Dr. Andreas Buchinger geleitet und steht für Ganzheitsmedizin und Naturheilverfahren.

Above the Kurzentrum, towards the north from Bergkurpark and Hirschpark, two renowned clinics are located at the foot of the Bomberg: The Psychosomatische Fachklinik (above), which utilises the many methods of therapy addressing inner well-being, is directly on Bombergallee. The Klinik Dr. Otto Buchinger (below), situated to the right of Bombergallee, family-run in the third generation now by Dr. Andreas Buchinger, stands for holistic medicine and natural remedies.

Am Hirschpark liegt die Hufeland-Therme. Lassen Sie sich verzaubern von der einzigartigen Atmosphäre, Entspannung pur. In der Nähe befindet sich das Rehazentrum Bad Pyrmont-Friedrichshöhe. Erst vor kurzem baulich erweitert, grundlegend saniert und restauriert, ist diese Anlage ein wunderbares Beispiel dafür, wie harmonisch sich drei historische Etappen vom Genesungsheim Friedrichshöhe 1901 bis heute zu einer zeitgemäßen Einheit zusammenfügen. Die DAK Fachklinik „Haus Weserland“ (rechts) am Ende des Vogelreichsweges ist ein weiteres Beispiel für die erfolgreiche Renovierung einer Fachklinik, die stets einen sehr guten Ruf bei den Gästen genießt.

Next to Hirschpark, the Hufeland-Therme thermal bath has its location. Get enchanted by its unique atmosphere promising perfect relaxation. Nearby, the Rehazentrum (rehabilitation centre) Bad Pyrmont Friedrichshöhe is to be found. Extended and fundamentally modernised and restored only recently, this facility is an excellent example of how harmoniously three different historic stages of architecture can be combined, from the original ‘Genesungsheim Friedrichshöhe’ (a convalescent home) of 1901 to the most recent additions. The DAK Fachklinik ‘Haus Weserland’ (above) at the end of Vogelreichsweg, yet another example of successful renovation, is a specialist clinic with a very good reputation among clients.

Einen hervorragenden medizinischen Ruf der Bad Pyrmonter Klinik-Einrichtungen besitzen auch die am Rande des Kurzentrums in Richtung Holzhausen gelegenen Einrichtungen. Zu nennen sind das Rehazentrum Bad Pyrmont, Therapiezentrum Brunswiek (oben links) sowie das dazugehörige Rehazentrum Bad Pyrmont „Klinik Weser" (unten links) und die m&i-Fachklinik (oben rechts). In Richtung Löwensen liegt das neu strukturierte und renovierte Ev. Bathildiskrankenhaus (unten rechts).

The excellent medical reputation of Bad Pyrmont therapeutic establishments is also shared by the facilities situated on the edge of the Kurzentrum towards Holzhausen. This applies in particular to the Rehazentrum Bad Pyrmont, Therapiezentrum Brunswiek (top left), and the m&i-Fachklinik (top right), to the Rehazentrum Bad Pyrmont 'Klinik Weser (bottom left)', and of course also to the Ev. Bathildiskrankenhaus (bottom right), fundamentally restructured and renovated over a period of several years, in the direction of Löwensen.

Vier Gotteshäuser prägen das kirchliche Leben in der Stadt:

Die katholische Kirche St. Georg wurde von 1903 bis 1905 im gotischen Stil errichtet (links).

Die ev. Johanniskirche im Ortsteil Holzhausen (oben rechts) wurde 1953–54 erbaut.

Der Architekt Wilhelm Hase aus Hannover hat ab 1880 die auf romanische Vorbilder zurückreichende ev. St. Petri-Kirche im Ortsteil Oesdorf geplant (unten rechts).

Die neugotische Stadtkirche (rechts Seite 51) oberhalb des Brunnenplatzes wurde nach Plänen des Architekten August Orth 1872–77 erbaut.

Four places of worship characterise religious life in town:

The Catholic church of St. Georg was constructed between 1903 and 1905 in Gothic style (Page 50, left).

The Protestant Johanniskirche in the district of Holzhausen (top left) was built 1953–54.

Starting in 1880, and basing his work on Roman-style examples, architect Wilhelm Hase of Hannover designed the Protestant St.-Petri-Kirche in the district of Oesdorf (bottom left).

The neo-Gothic Stadtkirche (right) above the Brunnenplatz was constructed 1872–77 according to designs by architect August Orth.

Sport und Freizeit
Sports and Leisure

Bad Pyrmont bietet seit Jahrhunderten eine erstklassige medizinische sowie ärztliche Versorgung. Gleiches gilt aber auch für das kulturelle Angebot. Musik, Theater, Bildende Künste dienen der seelischen Regeneration. Das Freizeitangebot ist außerordentlich vielfältig. Die Hufeland-Therme bietet sich an zum körperlichen Check-up, der Nordic Walking Park zwischen Königsberg und Bomberg ist anspruchsvoll, Fahrradvermietungen ermöglichen gut beschilderte Radausflüge, das Erlebnisbad „Die Welle“ fordert den Schwimmer heraus, Tennis und Golf können in schönster Landschaft ausgeübt werden.

For centuries, Bad Pyrmont has been offering first-class medical care and attendance. The same standards also apply to the cultural offers: music, theatre, graphic and visual arts are stimulants for inner regeneration. The range of leisure offers is extremely varied. For a physical check-up, the Hufeland-Therme offers itself, the Nordic Walking Park between Königsberg and Bomberg is demanding, bicycle rentals provide the means to cycling tours on well-signposted paths, the event bath ‘Die Welle’ challenges swimmers, and there are tennis and golf facilities in the beautiful landscape.

An extensive network of hiking trails makes the beauty of the landscape around Pyrmont accessible. Already in 1772, Johann Gottfried Herder wrote to his fiancée: „Ich bin jetzt auf dem Lande, in der schönsten Deutschesten, Romantischsten Gegend von der Welt" ("I am now in the countryside, in the loveliest, most German, most romantic spot in the world").

Ein ausgedehntes Wanderwegenetz erschließt die Schönheit der Pyrmonter Landschaft. Schon Johann Gottfried Herder schrieb 1772 an seine Braut „Ich bin jetzt auf dem Lande, in der schönsten Deutschesten, Romantischsten Gegend von der Welt".

Ein beliebter Wanderweg führt über die Bombergallee hinauf zum Bomberg oder alternativ entlang der Waldgrenze auf dem Philosophenweg in Richtung Erdfälle , ein anderer Weg führt hinauf zum Spelunkenturm (rechts unten), ein dritter schließlich leitet den Wanderer in östlicher Richtung über den Schellenturm zum Langen Grund. Vom Schellenturm wie vom Spelunkenturm hat man eindrucksvolle Blicke hinunter in das Tal. Der restaurierte Schellenturm erinnert zugleich an die Burganlage aus dem 12. Jahrhundert, an die früheste Besiedlung des Tales. Alle drei Wanderangebote können ein Ausflugslokal zum Ziel haben.

One popular hiking trail leads along Bombergallee up to the Bomberg or alternatively along the forest edge on Philosophenweg in the direction of the Erdfälle, another one leads uphill to the Spelunkenturm (bottom right), yet a third one leads hikers in an easterly direction via the Schellenturm to Langer Grund. On all three trails, it is possible to arrange the route for catering to be available at the end point.

Wandermöglichkeiten bieten sich in jeder Himmelsrichtung. Der Oesberg wurde nach dem Aufenthalt des preußischen Königs Friedrich II. in „Königsberg“ umbenannt. Er ist gekrönt vom Bismarckturm. Durch die Emmerwiesen, gleichsam auf den Spuren Goethes, der diesen Weg besonders liebte, gelangt man nach Lügde in eine Ackerbürgerstadt mit sehenswerten Fachwerkhäusern. Bis zum Jahr 1668, bis zum so genannten Hauptvergleich zwischen dem Fürstenhaus Waldeck und dem Bischof von Paderborn, bildeten Pyrmont und Lügde eine Einheit. Seit diesem Datum befinden sich zwei Herrschaften in diesem Tal, heute sind es Nordrhein-Westfalen und Niedersachsen.

There are all kinds of possibilities for hikes in all directions. The Oesberg was renamed ‘Königsberg’ (‘King’s Mountain’) after Prussian King Frederick II. stayed here. It is crowned by the pinnacle of the Bismarckturm. Through the Emmerwiesen, as if in the footsteps of Goethe, who loved this path very much, one gets to Lügde, a town of citizen farmers with remarkable half-timbered houses. Up to the year 1668, until the so-called Hauptvergleich (‘main settlement’) between the princely House of Waldeck and the bishop of Paderborn, Pyrmont and Lügde formed one administrative unit. Since that date, two lords have been ruling this valley, and nowadays, the division is between the states of Nordrhein-Westfalen and Niedersachsen.

Wandert man in westlicher Richtung, gelangt man von Pyrmont aus durch das ehemalige Dorf Holzhausen, durch Wälder und Wiesenflächen zum Dorf Hagen, das in schöner Lage oberhalb des Tales thront. Von hier hat man nicht nur einen schönen Blick über den Pyrmonter Talkessel, sondern auch in die weite Landschaft des benachbarten Lipperlandes. Unten: Hamborner Mühle, schon von Königin Luise besucht, liegt an der Landesgrenze.

Walking towards the east from Pyrmont, through the former village of Holzhausen and then lovely forests and meadows, one gets to the village of Hagen, in a beautiful location above the valley. From here, the view includes not only the round of the Pyrmont valley, but also the wide expanse of the neighbouring Lippe area.
Below: Hamborner Mühle.

Blick auf Bad Pyrmont aus östlicher Richtung. Am Fuße des Königsberges ist sowohl Löwensen in Teilen erkennbar als auch die ehemalige Quäkersiedlung Friedensthal. Der Bismarckturm auf dem Königsberg ist gut erkennbar. Das Kurzentrum mit dem Kurpark wird eingerahmt von den Ortsteilen Oesdorf und Holzhausen. Der Ortsteil Hagen ist in der Ferne zu entdecken. In der Kernstadt wohnen heute etwa 17.000 Einwohner.

A view of Bad Pyrmont from the east. At the foot of the Königsberg, parts of Löwensen as well as the former Quaker settlement of Friedensthal can be recognised. The Bismarckturm on top of the Königsberg can be seen clearly. The Kurzentrum and Kurpark are framed by the districts of Oesdorf and Holzhausen. The district of Hagen can be made out in the distance. The central part of town nowadays has a population of approx. 17,000.

Auf der Ottensteiner Hochebene zählen die fünf Dörfer Neersen, Baarsen, Kleinenberg, Großenberg und Eichenborn seit Jahrhunderten zum Fürstentum Waldeck-Pyrmont. Die Hochebene ist von bemerkenswerter Schönheit, die Kirche in Neersen ist unbedingt einen Besuch wert. In Kleinenberg befindet sich auch der Flugplatz für Sportflugzeuge.

The five villages of Neersen, Baarsen, Kleinenberg, Großenberg and Eichenborn on the high plain of Ottenstein have been part of the Princedom of Waldeck-Pyrmont for centuries. The high plain is of remarkable beauty, and the church of Neersen is definitely worth a visit. There is also an airfield for small planes in Kleinenberg.

Landschaft und Ausflugsziele
The Landscape and Sights to Visit

Ausflüge in die Landschaft rund um den Kurort Bad Pyrmont sind lohnenswert. Der Emmerfluss zieht mäanderartig durch die Landschaft Lippe und Weserbergland in Richtung Weser. Auf der Höhe von Schieder wurde die Emmer, die später auch an Lügde und Bad Pyrmont vorbeifließt, in den Jahren 1982–83 auf einer Länge von 3,5 km aufgestaut. Vor allen Dingen die Wassersportinteressierten finden hier viele Möglichkeiten.

Outings into the landscape surrounding the spa town of Bad Pyrmont are worth it. The river Emmer meanders through the Lippe and Weser Mountain countryside towards the river Weser. At the level of Schieder, the Emmer, which further down also passes Lügde and Bad Pyrmont, was dammed up in 1982–83 over a distance of 3.5 km. Especially watersports enthusiasts will find many interesting possibilities here.

Wer Lügde bei einer solchen Wanderung näher kennenlernen möchte, dem ist auch eine Besichtigung der romanischen Kilianskirche aus der Zeit Karls des Großen zu empfehlen. Ein Rundgang um die mit Stadtmauern und Türmen umbaute Stadt gibt viele Eindrücke von Lügde. Der Osterräderlauf am Abend des Ostersonntages ist ein einzigartiges Erlebnis.

Those who want to get to know Lügde a little better on such a walk should also take a look at the Roman-style Kilianskirche built in the days of Charlemagne. A tour around the town framed by walls and towers provides many impressive views of Lügde. The event of the 'Osterräderlauf' on the eve of Easter Sunday is something unique to be experienced.

Schloss Hämelschenburg, eines der schönsten Schlösser der Weserrenaissance, ist ein besonderes architektonisches Juwel am Emmerfluss. Dieses sehenswerte Bauwerk der Renaissance, 1551 bis 1609 errichtet von Jürgen von Klenke, ist von Bad Pyrmont aus gut mit dem Fahrrad entlang der Emmer zu erreichen.
Schloss Hämelschenburg, one of the most beautiful palaces of the Weser Renaissance, is an extraordinary architectural gem on the river Emmer. This noteworthy Renaissance building, constructed between 1551 and 1609 by Jürgen von Klenke, can be reached easily from Bad Pyrmont by bicycle along the Emmer.

Unmittelbar neben dem Informationszentrum: Erlebnis-Zoo Bad Pyrmont. Besucher können viele Tiere aus nächster Nähe beobachten.
Next to the Informationszentrum: Bad Pyrmont Adventure Zoo. Visitors can see lots of animals at close quarters.

Anlaufstelle für alle Gäste von Bad Pyrmont ist das Informationszentrum am Ende der Unteren Hauptallee. Der transparente Glasbau, geformt aus einem Achteck, nimmt die Architektur des Brunnentempels auf dem Brunnenplatz wieder auf und befindet sich so in Blickkontakt mit dem ehrwürdigen Gebäude auf dem Brunnenplatz, wo die Geschichte des Badeortes und der Heilquellen vor 2000 Jahren begonnen hatte.
The place of orientation for all guests to Bad Pyrmont is the Informationszentrum at the end of Untere Hauptallee. The transparent, octagonal glass construction recreates the architecture of the fountain temple on Brunnenplatz, thus establishing a visible link to the venerable building on Brunnenplatz in the place where the history of the spa town and the medicinal springs began 2,000 years ago.

Ausbildungsstätten und bedeutende Arbeitgeber
Training Institutions and Major Employers

The foundation for professional rehabilitation of the State of Lower Saxony has existed since 1980, its institutions for professional training (Berufsförderungswerke) in Bad Pyrmont and Weser-Ems in Bookholzberg were established over 60 years ago. Their purpose is to provide job prospects and measures for a start in a new profession to people who are unable or will soon become unable to practise their original profession for health reasons. The origins of the Berufsförderungswerk in Bad Pyrmont can be found in the Bundesversehrtenfachschule (federal vocational college for invalids) established in 1947 on the premises of Pyrmont Palace and the Kommandantenhaus.

Die Stiftung des Landes Niedersachsen für berufliche Rehabilitation betreut die Berufsförderungswerke in Bad Pyrmont und Weser-Ems in Bookholzberg. Aufgabe ist es, Menschen, die aus gesundheitlichen Gründen ihren ursprünglichen Beruf jetzt oder in naher Zukunft nicht mehr ausüben können, Perspektiven anzubieten und Maßnahmen für einen beruflichen Neustart durchzuführen. Ausgangspunkt für das BfW in Bad Pyrmont war die Einrichtung einer Bundesversehrtenfachschule ab 1947 in den Räumen von Schloss und Kommandantenhaus Bad Pyrmont.

A spa town such as Bad Pyrmont is well advised to promote medium-sized businesses. Companies in the field of computer technology have been established in Holzhausen as well as in Löwensen – foremost examples being the company of Meinberg Funkuhren (right) and the company of Phoenix Contact Electronics.

Ein Kurort wie Bad Pyrmont ist gut beraten, mittelständische Unternehmen zu fördern. Firmen auf dem Gebiet der Computertechnologie haben sich in Holzhausen wie in Löwensen etabliert – die Firma Meinberg Funkuhren (oben) wie die Firma Phoenix Contact Electronics sind beste Beispiele dafür.

A Brief History of Bad Pyrmont

1st–4th century	worship of the Brodelbrunnen spring with sacrificial offerings. Cf. 'Pyrmonter Brunnenfund'
889	mentioned for the first time in a document, the 'Arnulf-Urkunde'
1184	County of Pyrmont founded
1526–1562	construction of Pyrmont Castle by the counts of Schwalenberg
1556/57	the 'Wundergeläuf'
1667/1668	as a consequence of the settlement named 'Pyrmontischer Hauptvergleich', Count Georg Friedrich von Waldeck-Pyrmont becomes regent of Pyrmont and immediately commissions a number of building measures to modernise the spa town, such as construction of the Hauptallee and a spring temple, establishment of Brunnenstraße
1681	'Summer of the Princes': meeting of the highest-ranking families of the northern German aristocracy
1706–1728	construction of the palace as the summer residence of the Princes of Waldeck und Pyrmont in baroque style on the premises of the Renaissance fortress
1705	oldest hand-written directory of spa guests
1716	important spa guests of the season are Tsar Peter the Great, the English King George I. and philosopher Gottfried Wilhelm Leibniz
1717	discovery of the Bergsäuerling spring
1720	city rights awarded to Neustadt Pyrmont
1744, 1746	Prussian king Frederick the Great stays for courses of treatment
1750–1781	extension of the system of avenues by the Hylligen Born Allee, Springbrunnenallee and Klosterallee
1801	Johann Wolfgang von Goethe stays at the spa
1806	Prussian queen Luise stays at Pyrmont for the third time, after 1777 and 1797
1867/68	construction of a cast-iron spring temple and an ambulatory on Brunnenplatz
1903–1905	the landscape garden established by Werner Dirks
From 1912	the palm garden established by Werner Dirks
1914	the town is renamed to Bad Pyrmont
1922	administrative union of the former Princedom of Pyrmont with Prussia
1923/24	consruction of the current ambulatory and the fountain temple above the Hylligen Born spring
1932–1935	design of the Mittlerer Kurpark and the Bergkurpark
1947	Bad Pyrmont officially recognised as a spa by the State of Lower Saxony
1978	opening of the Brunnenstraße pedestrian zone
1999	recognition as a world-wide Expo Project 'Aqua Bad Pyrmont' with far-reaching consequences, such as a new design for Brunnenplatz, Untere Hauptallee, Dunsthöhle and the medicinal springs
2001	reopening of the Hufelandtherme thermal bath after fire damage
2005	title of the most beautiful spa park in Germany awarded

Kleine Geschichte von Bad Pyrmont

1–4. Jahrhundert	Verehrung der Brodelbrunnenquelle durch Opfergaben. Pyrmonter Brunnenfund
889	Erste schriftliche Erwähnung in der Arnulf-Urkunde
1184	Gründung der Grafschaft Pyrmont
1526–1562	Bau der Festung Pyrmont durch die Grafen von Schwalenberg
1556/57	Das Wundergeläuf
1667/1668	Graf Georg Friedrich von Waldeck-Pyrmont wird im so genannten Pyrmontischen Hauptvergleich Regent in Pyrmont und beginnt sofort mit einer Reihe von Maßnahmen, um den Badeort zu modernisieren, unter anderem Anlage der Hauptallee, Bau eines Brunnentempels, Anlage der Brunnenstraße
1681	Fürstensommer: Treffpunkt der hochrangigsten Adelsfamilien aus dem norddeutschen Raum
1706–1728	Neubau des Schlosses als barocke Sommerresidenz der Fürsten zu Waldeck und Pyrmont auf dem Gelände der Renaissance-Festung
1705	Älteste handgeschriebene Kurliste
1716	Bedeutende Kurgäste in jener Saison sind Zar Peter der Große, der englische König Georg I. und der Philosoph Gottfried Wilhelm Leibniz
1717	Entdeckung der Bergsäuerlingsquelle
1720	Verleihung der Stadtrechte an die Neustadt Pyrmont
1744, 1746	Kuraufenthalte des preußischen Königs Friedrich der Große
1750–1781	Ausbau des Alleensystems mit Hylligen Born Allee, Springbrunnenallee und Klosterallee
1801	Johann Wolfgang von Goethe ist Kurgast
1806	ist die preußische Königin Luise zum dritten Male, nach 1777 und 1797, Kurgast in Pyrmont
1867/68	Bau eines gusseisernen Brunnentempels und einer Wandelhalle auf dem Brunnenplatz
1903–1905	Anlage des Landschaftsgartens durch Werner Dirks
Ab 1912	Anlage des Palmengartens durch Werner Dirks
1914	Erhält die Stadt den Namen Bad Pyrmont
1922	Anschluss des ehemaligen Fürstentums Pyrmont an Preußen
1923/24	Bau der heutigen Wandelhalle und des Brunnentempels über der Hylligen Born-Quelle.
1932–1935	Gestaltung des Mittleren Kurparks und des Bergkurparks
1947	Bad Pyrmont Niedersächsisches Staatsbad
1978	Einweihung des Fußgängerbereichs Brunnenstraße
1999	Anerkennung als weltweites Expo-Projekt „Aqua Bad Pyrmont“ mit weitreichenden Folgen für die Neugestaltung von Brunnenplatz, Unterer Hauptallee, Dunsthöhle und Heilquellen
2001	Wiedereröffnung der Hufelandtherme nach Brand
2005	Auszeichnung als schönster Kurpark Deutschlands

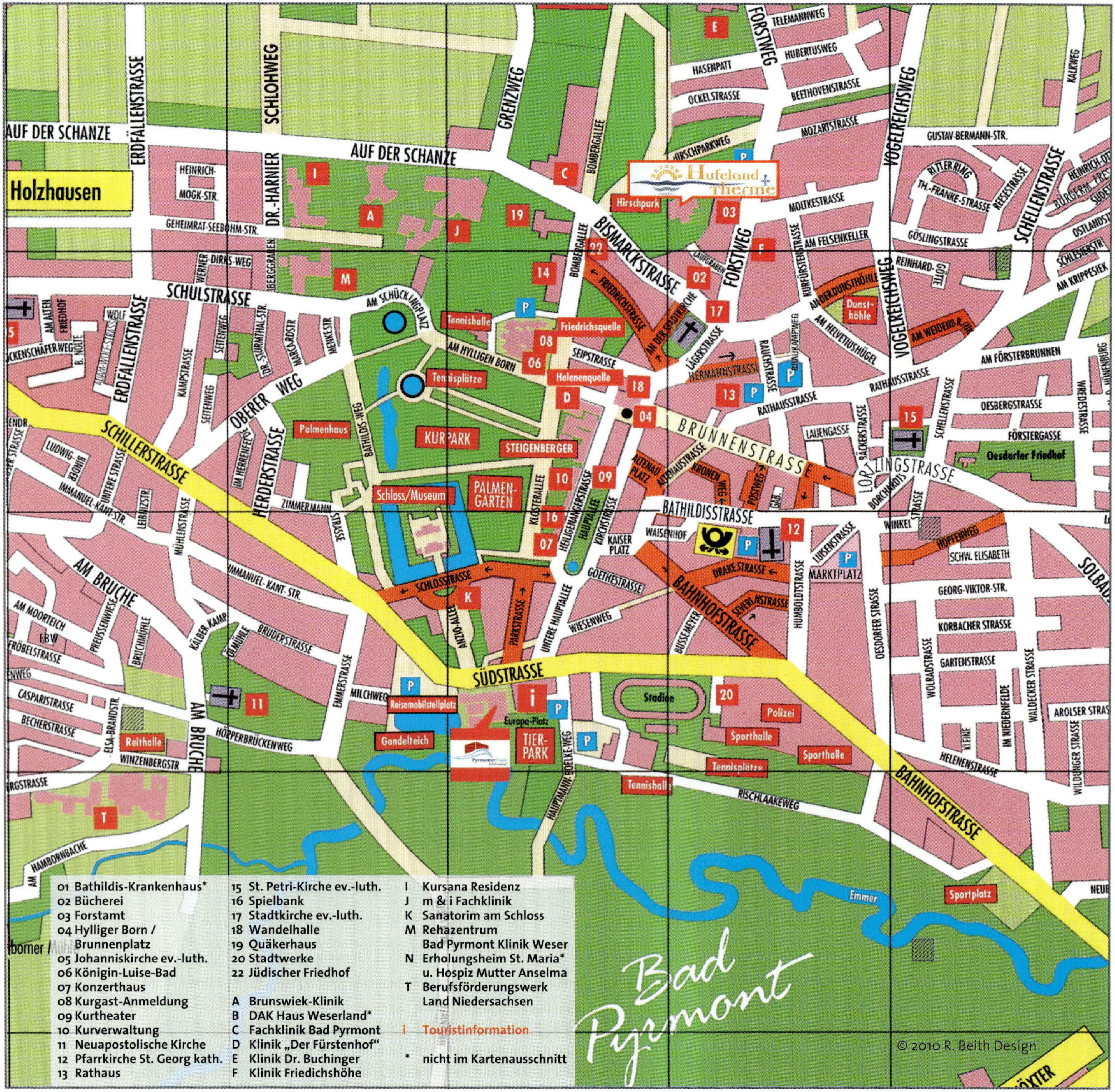
Holzhausen
AUF DER SCHANZE
ERDFÄLLENSTRASSE
SCHLOHWEG
GRENZWEG
BOMBERGALLEE
FORSTWEG
TELEMANNWEG
HUBERTUSWEG
HASENPATT
BEETHOVENSTRASSE
OCKELSTRASSE
MOZARTSTRASSE
VOGELREICHSWEG
KALKWEG
GUSTAV-BERMANN-STR.
SCHELLENSTRASSE
HIRSCHPARKWEG
Hufeland Therme
Hirschpark
HEINRICH-MOGK-STR.
DR.-HARNIER
GEHEIMRAT-SEEBOHM-STR.
BISMARCKSTRASSE
MOLTKESTRASSE
RITTERRING
TH.-FRANKE-STRASSE
GÖSLINGSTRASSE
AM FELSENKELLER
KURFÜRSTENSTRASSE
REINHARD-
OSTLANDSTR.
AM KRIPPESIEK
WERNER-DIRKS-WEG
BERGGRABEN
SCHULSTRASSE
FRIEDRICHSTRASSE
AM DER STADTKIRCHE
LÄGERSTRASSE
AN DER DUNSTHÖHLE
Dunsthöhle
AM WEIDENB.
AM HELVETIUSHÜGEL
AM FÖRSTERBRUNNEN
AM SCHÜCKINGPLATZ
Tennishalle
Friedrichsquelle
AM HYLLIGEN BORN
SEIPSTRASSE
HERMANNSTRASSE
Tennisplätze
Helenenquelle
RATHAUSSTRASSE
OESBERGSTRASSE
FÖRSTERGASSE
Oesdorfer Friedhof
AM ALTEN FRIEDHOF
WOLF
KAMPSTRASSE
SEITENWEG
OBERER WEG
Palmenhaus
KURPARK
STEIGENBERGER
BRUNNENSTRASSE
LAUENGASSE
LORTZINGSTRASSE
SCHILLERSTRASSE
HERDERSTRASSE
BATHILDIS-WEG
Schloss/Museum
PALMEN-GARTEN
KLOSTERALLEE
HEILIGENANGERSTRASSE
HAUPTALLEE
ALTENAU PLATZ
KRONEN
POSTWEG
BATHILDISSTRASSE
ZIMMERMANN STRASSE
LEIBNIZSTR.
MÜHLENSTRASSE
KAISER PLATZ
WAISENHOF
MARKTPLATZ
LUISENSTRASSE
WINKEL
HOPFENWEG
SCHW. ELISABETH
AM BRUCHE
IMMANUEL-KANT-STR.
SCHLOSSSTRASSE
GOETHESTRASSE
DRAKE-STRASSE
BAHNHOFSTRASSE
SEVERINSTRASSE
HUMBOLDTSTRASSE
GEORG-VIKTOR-STR.
KORBACHER STRASSE
GARTENSTRASSE
AM MOORTEICH
PREUSSENWIESE
FRÖBELSTRASSE
BRUDERSTRASSE
ANZIO-ALLEE
PARKSTRASSE
UNTERE HAUPTALLEE
WIESENWEG
BUSSEMEYER
OESDORFER STRASSE
SÜDSTRASSE
CASPARISTRASSE
BECHERSTRASSE
ELSA-BRANDSTR.
Reithalle
WINZENBERGSTR.
HÖPPERBRÜCKENWEG
AM BRUCHE
EMMERSTRASSE
MILCHWEG
Reisemobilstellplatz
Gondelteich
Europa-Platz
TIER-PARK
HAUPTMANN-BOELKE-WEG
Stadion
Polizei
Sporthalle
Sporthalle
Tennisplätze
Tennishalle
RISCHLAAKEWEG
WOLRADSTRASSE
IM NIEDERNFELDE
WALDECKER STRASSE
AROLSER STRASSE
HELENENSTRASSE
WILDUNGER STRASSE
BAHNHOFSTRASSE
HAMBORNBACHE
Emmer
Sportplatz
01 Bathildis-Krankenhaus*
02 Bücherei
03 Forstamt
04 Hylliger Born / Brunnenplatz
05 Johanniskirche ev.-luth.
06 Königin-Luise-Bad
07 Konzerthaus
08 Kurgast-Anmeldung
09 Kurtheater
10 Kurverwaltung
11 Neuapostolische Kirche
12 Pfarrkirche St. Georg kath.
13 Rathaus
15 St. Petri-Kirche ev.-luth.
16 Spielbank
17 Stadtkirche ev.-luth.
18 Wandelhalle
19 Quäkerhaus
20 Stadtwerke
22 Jüdischer Friedhof
A Brunswiek-Klinik
B DAK Haus Weserland*
C Fachklinik Bad Pyrmont
D Klinik „Der Fürstenhof“
E Klinik Dr. Buchinger
F Klinik Friedichshöhe
I Kursana Residenz
J m & i Fachklinik
K Sanatorim am Schloss
M Rehazentrum Bad Pyrmont Klinik Weser
N Erholungsheim St. Maria* u. Hospiz Mutter Anselma
T Berufsförderungswerk Land Niedersachsen
i Touristinformation
* nicht im Kartenausschnitt
Bad Pyrmont
© 2010 R. Beith Design
HÖXTER